Book 1
C++ Programming Professional
Made Easy

BY SAM KEY

&

Book 2
HTML Professional
Programming Made Easy

BY SAM KEY

Book 1
C++ Programming Professional Made Easy

BY SAM KEY

Expert C++ Programming Language Success in a Day for Any Computer User!

Table Of Contents

Introduction.. 5

Chapter 1 - Introduction to C++ 6

Chapter 2 - C++ Variables and Operators.. 11

Chapter 3 - All About User Input.. 17

Chapter 4 - Using Flow Control Statements 21

Conclusion 27

Introduction

I want to thank you and congratulate you for purchasing the book, "Professional C++ Programming Made Easy".

This book contains proven steps and strategies on how to learn the C++ programming language as well as its applications.

There's no need to be a professional developer to code quick and simple C++ programs. With this book, anyone with basic computer knowledge can explore and enjoy the power of the *C++ Programming Language.* Included are the following fundamental topics for any beginner to start coding *today:*

- The basic C++ terms

- Understanding the C++ Program Structure

- Working with Variables, Expressions, and Operators

- Using the Input and Output Stream for User Interaction

- Creating Logical Comparisons

- Creating Loops and Using Condition Statements

- And Many More!

Thanks again for purchasing this book, I hope you enjoy it!

Chapter 1 – Introduction to C++

What You Will Learn:

**A Brief History of the C++ Language

**C++ Basic Terminology

**C++ Program Structure

C++ is one of the most popular programming languages that people are using today. More specifically, C++ is a library of "commands" that tell your computer what to do and how to do it. These commands make up the *C++ source code.*

Take note that C++ is different from the *C* programming language that came before it. In fact, it is supposedly better version of the C language when *Bjarne Stroustrup* created it back in 1983.

Even today, the C++ language serves as the "starting point" for many experts in the world of programming. Although it is particularly easy to learn and apply, the ceiling for C++ mastery is incredibly high.

C++ Basic Terminology

Of course, the first step in learning the C++ programming language is to understand the basic terms. To prevent any unnecessary confusion at any point as you read this book, this section explains the most commonly used terms in the C++ program syntax. Just like the entire programming language itself, most terms in C++ are easy to remember and understand.

Compiler

Before anything else, take note that a compiler is needed to run the codes you've written with C++. Think of compilers as "translators" that convert programming language into *machine language* – the language that a computer understands. The machine language consists of only two characters (1s and 0s), which is why it is also called as *binary language*. If you're learning C++ at school, then you shouldn't worry about getting a compiler for C++ *or* an *Integrated Development Environment* for that matter.

Integrated Development Environment

An Integrated Development Environment (IDE) is essentially the software you're using to write C++ programs. It only makes sense for IDEs to come with compilers needed to run your codes. If you have no experience with C++ programming and attempting to learn it on your own, you can opt for a free C++ IDE such as *Code::Blocks*. A good choice for complete beginners is to opt for a simple C++ IDE such as *Quincy 2005* since there is very little setup required.

Variables and Parameters

Variables are individual blocks in the program's memory that contains a given value. A value may be set as a constant, determined by the value of other variables using operators, or set/changed through user input. Variables are denoted by variable names or *identifiers*. In programming with C++, you can use any variable name you desire as long as all characters are valid. Remember that only alphanumeric characters and "underscores" (_) can be used in identifiers. Punctuation marks and other symbols are not allowed.

Keep in mind that variables always need to be *declared* first before they can be used. Declaring variables are different from deciding their actual values; meaning both processes are done in two different codes. These processes will be explained in the next chapter.

"Parameters" work the same way as regular variables. In fact, they are even written in the same syntax. However, parameters and variables are initialized in different ways. Parameters are specifically included in *functions* to allow arguments to be passed to a separate location from which the functions are called.

Statements

Every program written with C++ consists of different lines of code that performs tasks such as setting variables, calling functions, and other expressions. These lines are *statements*. Each individual statement always ends with a semicolon (;). More importantly, statements in a function are executed chronologically based on which comes first. Of course, this order can be altered using *flow control statements* such as "if statements" and "loops".

Functions

Functions are blocks in a C++ program structured to complete a single task. You can call upon functions at any point whilst the program is running. Curly brackets or braces ({}) enclose the statements or "body" in each function. Aside from a function name, functions are also set with corresponding "types" which refer to the requested form of *returned value*. You can also use and set parameters at the beginning of each function. They are enclosed in parentheses "()" and separated using commas (,).

In C++, the following is the most used syntax when creating functions:

"type" "name" (parameter 1, parameter 2, parameter 3, ...)
{
        "statements";
}

Comments

When working on particularly bigger projects, most experienced programmers use "comments" that can be used as descriptions for specific sections in a C++ program. Comments are completely ignored by a compiler and can therefore ignore proper coding syntax. Comments are preceded either by a *two slashes* (//) or a *slash-asterisk* (/*). You will find comments in the examples throughout this book to help you understand them. A quick example would be the *"Hello World!"* program below. Of course, you can also use comments in your future projects for reference and debugging purposes.

The C++ Program Structure

The program structure of C++ is very easy to understand. The compiler reads every line of code from top to bottom. This is why the first part of a C++ program usually starts with *preprocessor directives* and the declaration of variables and their values. The best way to illustrate this structure is to use the most popular example in the world of C++ -- the "Hello World!" program. Take note of the lines of code as well as the comments below:

#include <iostream> // this is a preprocessor directive

int main() // this line initiates the function named main, which should be found in every C++ program

{

> **std::cout << "Hello World!";** // the statements found between the curly braces make up the main function's body

> **return 0;** // the return 0; statement is required to tell the program that the function ran correctly. However, some compilers do not require this line in the main function

}

The topmost line ("#include <iostream>") is a preprocessor directive that defines a section of the standard C++ programming library known as the Input/Output Stream or simply *iostream*. This section handles the input and output operations in C++ programs. Remember that this is important if you wish to use "std::cout" in the main function's body.

The first line "int main ()" initializes the main function. Remember that the "int" refers to the *integer* data type and he "main" refers to the function's name. There are other data types aside from int. But you should focus on the integer data type for now. Since the "Hello World!" program does not need a parameter, it leaves the space between the parentheses succeeding the function name blank. Also, bear in mind that you should NOT place a semicolon (;) after initializing functions.

Next is the function's body, denoted by the open curly brace. This particular part ("std::cout") of the program refers to the **st**andard **c**haracter **out**put device, which is the computer's display device. Next comes the *insertion operator* (<<) from the input/output stream which means the rest of the line is to be outputted (excluding quotations). Lastly, the statement is closed with a semicolon (;).

The last line in the function's body is the *return statement* ("return = 0;"). Remember that the return expression (in this example, "0") depends on the data type specified upon initialization of the function. However, it is possible to create functions without the need for return statements using the "void" function type. For example; *void main ()*.

An alternate way to do this is to include the line "using namespace std;" under the preprocessor line so you no longer need to write "std::" each time you use it. If you opt for this method, the code would look like:

#include <iostream>

using namespace std;

int main()

{

    cout << "Hello World!";

    return 0;

}

Chapter 2 – C++ Variables and Operators

What You Will Learn:

**Introduction to C++ Operators and How to Use Them

**Declaring and Determining the Value of Variables

**Creating New Lines in the Program Output

In a C++ program, variables and constants are controlled or "operated" using *Operators*. Take note that the basic operators in the C++ programming language are essentially the same as arithmetic operator. This includes the equal sign (=) for assigning expressions, the plus sign (+) for addition, the minus sign (-) for subtraction, the asterisk (*) for multiplication, the forward slash (/) for division, and the percentage sign (%) for obtaining the remainder from any expression.

C++ also uses other operators to fulfill additional tasks other than basic arithmetic operations. As mentioned in the previous chapter, the iostream header allowed you to use the insertion operator (<<) for processing output. There are also different operators accessible even without the #include directive. These "basic" operators can be categorized under *increment/decrement operators, comparison operators, compound assignment operators,* and *logical operators.*

Declaring Variables

Before using variables in C++ operations, you must first declare them and determine their values. Again, declaring variables and giving their values are two separate processes. The syntax for declaring variables are as follows:

"type" "variable";

Just like when initializing functions, you need to specify the data type to be used for a given variable. For example; say you want to declare "x" as an integer variable. The initialization should look like this:

int x;

After the declaration of x, you can give it a value using the assign operator (=). For example; to assign the value "99" to variable x, use the following line:

x = 99;

Make sure to declare a variable first before you assign a value to it. Alternatively, you can declare a variable and assign a value to it using a single line. This can be done using:

int x = 99;

Aside from setting these expressions as you write the program, you can also use operations and user input to determine their values as the program runs. But first, you need to learn about the other operators in C++.

Increment and Decrement Operators

The increment operator consists of two plus signs (++) while the decrement operator consists of two minus signs (--). The main purpose of increment and decrement operators is to shorten the expression of adding and subtracting 1 from any given variable. For example; if x = 2, then ++x should equal 3 while –x should equal 1.

If being used to determine the values of two or more variables, increment and decrement operators can be included as either a prefix or suffix. When used as a suffix (x++ or x--), it denotes the original value of x *before* adding or subtracting 1. When run on their own, both ++x and x++ have the same meaning. But when used in setting other variables, the difference is made obvious. Here is a simple example to illustrate the difference:

X = 5;

Y = ++x;

In this example, the value of y is determined *after* increasing the value of x. In other words, the value of y in this example is equal to 6.

X = 5;

Y = x++;

In this example, the value of y is determined *before* increasing the value of x. In other words, the value of y in this example is equal to 6.

Compound Assignment Operators

Aside from basic arithmetic operators and the standard assignment operator (=), compound assignment operators can also be used to perform an operation before a value is assigned. Compound assignment operators are basically shortened versions of normal expressions that use basic arithmetic operators.

Here are some examples of compound assignment operators:

x -= 1; // this is the same as the expression x = x – 1;

x *= y; // this is the same as the expression x = x * y;

x += 1;   // this is the same as the expression x = x + 1;

x /= y;   // this is the same as the expression x = x / y;

Comparison Operators

Variables and other expressions can be compared using relational or comparison operators. These operators are used to check whether a value is greater than, less than, or equal to another. Here are the comparison operators used in C++ and their description:

==   -   checks if the values are equal

<   -   checks if the first value is less than the second

>   -   checks if the first value is greater than the second

<=   -   checks if the first value is less than *or* equal to the second

>=   -   checks if the first value is greater than *or* equal to the second

!=   -   checks if the values are NOT equal

Comparison operators are commonly used in creating condition statements. They can also be used to evaluate an expression and return a *Boolean value* ("true" or "false"). Using the comparison operators listed above; here are some example expressions and their corresponding Boolean value:

(8 == 1) // this line evaluates to "false"

(8 > 1) // this line evaluates to "true"

(8 != 1) // this line evaluates to "true"

(8 <= 1) // this line evaluates to "false"

Also take note that the Boolean value "false" is equivalent to "0" while "true" is equivalent to other non-zero integers.

Aside from numerical values, the value of variables can also be checked when using comparison operators. Simply use a variable's identifier when creating the expression. Of course, the variable must be declared and given an identified value first before a valid comparison can be made. Here is an example scenario

```
#include <iostream>
using namespace std;

int main ()

{
        int a = 3;      // the values of a and b are set first
        int b = 4;
        cout << "Comparison a < b = " << (a < b);
        return 0;
}
```

The output for this code is as follows:

Comparison a < b = true

Take note that the insertion operator (<<) is used to insert the value of the expression "a < b" in the output statement, which is denoted in the 7th line ("cout << "Comparison a < b = "...). Don't forget that you *need an output statement* in order to see if your code works. The following code will produce no errors, but it won't produce an output either:

#include <iostream>

int main (

{

    int a = 3;
    int b = 4;
    (a < b);
    return 0;

}

In this code, it is also true that a < b. However, no output will be produced since the lines necessary for the program output are omitted.

Logical Operators

There are also other logical operators in C++ that can determine the values of Boolean data. They are the NOT (!), AND (&&), and OR (||) operators. Here are specific examples on how they are used:

!(6 > 2) // the **NOT** operator (!) completely reverses any relational expressions and produces the opposite result. This expression is false because 6 > 2 is correct

(6 > 2 && 5 < 10) // the **AND** (&&) operator only produces true if both expressions correct. This expression is true because both 6 > 2 && 5 < 10 are correct

(6 = 2 || 5 < 10) // the **OR** (||) operator produces true if one of the expressions are correct. This expression is true because the 5 < 10 is correct although 6 = 2 is false.

You can also use the NOT operator in addition to the other two logical operators. For example:

!(6 = 2 || 5 < 10) // this expression is false

!(6 > 2 && 5 < 10) // this expression is also false

!(6 < 2 && 5 < 10) // this expression is true

Creating New Lines

From this point on in this book, you will be introduced to simple C++ programs that produce output with multiple lines. To create new lines when producing output, all you need to do is to use the *new line character* (\n). Alternatively, you can use the "endl;" manipulator to create new lines when using the "cout" code. The main difference is that the *internal buffer* for the output stream is "flushed" whenever you use the "endl;" manipulator with "cout". Here are examples on how to use both:

cout << "Sentence number one \nSentence number two";

The example above uses the new line character.

cout << "Sentence number one" << endl;
cout << "Sentence number two";

The example above uses "endl;".

Of course, the first code (using \n) is relatively simpler and easier for general output purposes. Both will produce the following output:

Sentence number one

Sentence number two

Chapter 3 – All About User Input

What You Will Learn:

**Utilizing the Input Stream

**Using Input to Determine or Modify Values

**How to Input and Output Strings

Up to this point, you've learned how to make a C++ program that can perform arithmetic operations, comparisons, and can produce output as well. This time, you will learn how to code one of the most important aspects of computer programs – *user input.*

As stated earlier, user input can be utilized to determine or modify the values of certain variables. C++ programs use abstractions known as *streams* to handle input and output. Since you already know about the syntax for output ("cout"), it's time to learn about the syntax for input ("cin").

The Extraction Operator

The input syntax "cin" is used with the *extraction operator* (>>) for formatted input. This combination along with the *keyboard* is the standard input for most program environments. Remember that you still need to declare a variable first before input can be made. Here is a simple example:

int x; // this line declares the variable identifier x. Take note of the data type "int" which means that only an integer value is accepted

cin >> x;   // this line extracts input from the cin syntax and stores it to x

User input can also be requested for multiple variables in a single line. For example; say you want to store integer values for variables x and y. This should look like:

int x, y;   // this line declares the two variables

cin >> x >> y;   // this line extracts user input for variables x and y

Take note that the program will automatically require the user to input *two* values for the two variables. Which comes first depends on the order of the variables in the line (in this case, input for variable "x" is requested first).

Here is an example of a program that extracts user input and produces an output:

#include <iostream>   // again, this is essential for input and output
using namespace std;

int main ()

{

    int x;
    cout << "Insert a random number \n";
    cin >> x;   // this is where user input is extracted
    cout << "You inserted: " << x;
    return 0;

}

Bear in mind that the value extracted from the input stream overwrites any initial value of a variable. For example, if the variable was declared as "int x = 2;" but was later followed by the statement "cin >> x;", the new value will then replace the original value until the program/function restarts or if an assignment statement is introduced.

Strings

Keep in mind that there are other types you can assign to variables in C++. Aside from integers, another fundamental type is the *string*. A string is basically a variable type that can store sets of characters in a specific sequence. In other words, this is how you can assign words or sentences as values for certain variables.

First of all, you need to add the preprocessor directive "#include <string>" before you can use strings in your program. Next, you need to declare a string before it can receive assignments. For example; if you want to declare a string for "Name" and assign a value for it, you can use the code:

#include <string>
using namespace std;

int main ()

{
  string name;
  name = "Insert your name here"; // including quotations

}

Creating output using strings is basically the same as with integers. You only need to use "cout" and insert the string to the line. The correct syntax is as follows:

string name;

Name = "Your Name Here";

cout << "My name is: " << name;

Without any changes, the output for the above code is:

Your Name Here

Inputting Strings

To allow user input values for strings, you need to use the function "getline" in addition to the standard input stream "cin". The syntax for this is "getline (cin, [string]);". Below is an example program that puts string input into application.

```cpp
#include <iostream>
#include <string>
using namespace std;

int main ()

{
    string name;
    cout << "Greetings! What is your name?\n";
    getline (cin, name); // this is the extraction syntax
    cout << "Welcome " << name;
    return 0;

}
```

Take note that strings have "blank" values by default. This means nothing will be printed if no value is assigned or if there is no user input.

Chapter 4 – Using Flow Control Statements

What You Will Learn:

**If and Else Selection Statements

**Creating Choices

**Creating Iterating/Looping Statements

Remember that statements are the basic building blocks of a program written using C++. Each and every line that contains expressions such as a variable declaration, an operation, or an input extraction is a statement.

However, these statements are *linear* without some form of flow control that can establish the "sense" or "logic" behind a C++ program. This is why you should learn how to utilize flow control statements such as *selection statements* and *looping statements*.

If and Else Statements

If and else statements are the most basic form of logic in a C++ program. Basically, the main purpose of an "if" statement is to allow the execution of a specific line or "block" of multiple statements only *if* a specified condition is fulfilled.

Next is the "else" statement which allows you to specify what would occur in case the conditions aren't met. Without an "else" statement, everything inside the "if" statement will be completely ignored. Here the syntax for an "if" and "else" statement:

if (age >= 18)

      cout << "You are allowed to drink.";

else

cout << "You are not yet allowed to drink.";

Remember that conditions can only be set using comparison operators and logical operators (refer to Chapter 2). Take note that you can also execute multiple statements using if/else conditions by enclosing the lines in curly braces. It is also possible to use composite conditions using logical operators such as AND (&&) and OR (||).

Finally, you can use another "if" statement after an "else" statement for even more possibilities. Of course, you also need to specify conditions for every "if" statement you use. Here is a good example that demonstrates what you can do using "if" and "else" statements in addition to user input:

```cpp
#include <iostream>
using namespace std;

int main()

{
    int number;
    cout << "Enter a number from 1-3\n";
    cin >> number;
    if (number == 1 || number == 2)
        cout << "You have entered either 1 or 2.";
    else if (number == 3)
        cout << "You have entered 3.";
    else
    {
        cout << "Please follow the instructions\n";
        cout << "Please Try Again.";
    }
    return 0;
}
```

There are 3 possible outcomes in the program above. The first outcome is achieved if the user entered any of the numbers 1 or 2. The second outcome is achieved if the user entered the number 3. Lastly, the third outcome is achieved if the user entered a different number other the ones specified.

Creating Choices (Yes or No)

Another way to utilize if/else statements is to create "Yes or No" choices. For this, you need to make use of the variable type "char" which can hold a character from the *8-bit character set* (you can use char16_t, char32_t, or wchar_t for larger character sets; but this is not usually necessary). Just like all other variables, a "char" variable needs to be declared before it can be used.

Of course, you want the user to make the choice, which is why you need to use the "cin" function to extract user input. Here is a simple program that asks for the user's gender:

```
#include <iostream>
using namespace std;

int main()

{
        char gender; // this is the char variable declaration
        cout << "Male or Female? (M/F)";
        cin >> gender; // user input is stored to gender
        if (gender == 'm' || gender == 'M')
                cout << "You have selected Male.";
        else if (gender == 'f' || gender == 'F')
                cout << "You have selected Female.";
        else
                cout << "Please follow the instructions.";
        return 0;

}
```

Take note that you should use *single quotation marks* (') when pinpointing "char" values. In C++, "char" values are always called inside single quotation marks. Additionally, remember that "char" values are case-sensitive, which is why the example above used the OR (||) operator in the conditions to accept both lowercase and uppercase answers. You can see that the program above checked if the user entered 'm', 'M', 'f', or 'F'.

Looping Statements

Lastly, using "loops" allow statements to be executed for a set number of times or until a condition is met. By incorporating other statements in loops, you can do far more than just create pointless repetitions. But first, you need to be familiar with the different types of loops.

There are 3 types of loops in C++ -- *while, do,* and *for.*

While Loop

The *"while loop"* is regarded as the simplest form of loop in the C++. Basically, it repeats the statement(s) as long as the given condition is true. Keep in mind that your code should be structured to eventually fulfill the condition; otherwise you might create an "infinite loop".

Here is an example of a while loop:

```
int x = 100;

while (x >= 0)     // the condition for the loop is set
    {
    cout << x;
    --x;   // the value of x is decreased
    }
```

In this example, the loop executes as long as the value of x is greater than or equal to 0. Take note of the decrement operator (--) in the statement "--x;". This makes sure that the value of x is continually decreased until the condition is met and the loop ends.

Do-While Loop

The next type of loop is the *"do-while loop"*. The do-while loop is essentially the same as the while loop. The main difference is that the do-while loop allows the execution of the statement(s) at least *once* before the condition is checked. Whereas in the while loop, the condition is checked *first*.

Here is an example of a do-while loop:

```
int x = 100;
int y;

do
    {
    cout << "The value is " << x << "\n";
    cout << "Enter a value to subtract.";
    cin >> y;
    x -= y;
    }
while (x > 0);      // in the do-while loop, the condition is checked last
```

In the example above, the statements are executed at least once before the value of x is checked. Whereas in a while loop, there is a possibility that the statement(s) will not be executed at all.

For Loop

The third type of loop is the *"for loop"* which has specific areas for the *initialization, condition,* and *increase.* These three sections are sequentially executed throughout the life cycle of the loop. By structure, for loops are created to run a certain number of times because increment or decrement operators are usually used in the "increase" section.

Here is the syntax for this loop to help you understand it better:

for (int x = 10; x > 0; x--)

Notice the three expressions inside the parentheses (int x = 10; x > 0; x--) are separated in semicolons. These parameters denote the three sections of the loop. You may also use multiple expressions for each section using a comma (,). Here is the syntax for this:

for (int x = 10, y = 0; x != y; --x, ++y)

    {

    cout << "X and Y is different\n";

    }

In this example, the loop is executed as long as x is not equal to y. And in order for the loop to end, the values of x and y are adjusted until the value of x equals the value of y. Based on the parameters above, the statement "X and Y is different" will run a total of 5 times before the loop is ended.

Conclusion

Thank you again for purchasing this book!

I hope this book was able to help you to learn and understand the C++ programming language!

The next step is to start from where you are now and try to learn something new. Keep in mind that you've only scratched the surface of all the things you can do in the world of C++!

Finally, if you enjoyed this book, please take the time to share your thoughts and post a review on Amazon. We do our best to reach out to readers and provide the best value we can. Your positive review will help us achieve that. It'd be greatly appreciated!

Thank you and good luck!

Book 2
HTML Professional
Programming Made Easy

BY SAM KEY

Expert HTML Programming
Language Success in a Day for any
Computer Users

Table Of Contents

Introduction.. 30

Chapter 1: Getting Started with HTML 31

Chapter 2: Elements, Properties, Tags, and Attributes.................... 34

Chapter 3: The Standard Structure of HTML 39

Chapter 4: More HTML Tags... 42

Conclusion 47

Check Out My Other Books 48

Introduction

I want to thank you and congratulate you for purchasing the book, *Professional HTML Programming Made Easy: Expert HTML Programming Language Success In A Day for any Computer User!*

This book contains proven steps and strategies on how to create a web page in just a day. And if you have a lot of time in a day, you will be able to create a decent and informative website in two or three days.

HTML programming or development lessons are sometimes used as an introductory resource to programming and is a prerequisite to learning web development. In this book, you will be taught of the fundamentals of HTML. Mastering the contents of this book will make web development easier for you and will allow you to grasp some of the basics of computer programming.

To get ready for this book, you will need a desktop or laptop. That is all. You do not need to buy any expensive HTML or website development programs. And you do not need to rent a server or subscribe to a web hosting service. If you have questions about those statements, the answers are in the book.

Thanks again for purchasing this book. I hope you enjoy it!

Chapter 1: Getting Started with HTML

This book will assume that you have no prior knowledge on HTML. Do not skip reading any chapters or this book if you plan to learn about CSS, JavaScript, or any other languages that is related to web development.

HTML is a markup language. HTML defines what will be displayed on your browser and how it will be displayed. To program or code HTML, all you need is a text editor. If your computer is running on a Windows operating system, you can use Notepad to create or edit HTML files. Alternatively, if your computer is a Mac, you can use TextEdit instead.

Why is this book telling you to use basic text editors? Why are expert web developers using HTML creation programs such as Adobe Dreamweaver to create their pages? Those programs are supposed to make HTML coding easier, right?

You do not need them yet. Using one will only confuse you, especially if you do not know the fundamentals of HTML. Aside from that, web designing programs such as Adobe Dreamweaver are not all about dragging and dropping items on a web page. You will also need to be capable of manually writing the HTML code that you want on your page. That is why those programs have different views like Design and Code views. And most of them time, advanced developers stay and work more using the Code view, which is similar to a typical text editing program.

During your time learning HTML using this book, create a folder named HTML on your desktop. As you progress, you will see snippets of HTML code written here. You can try them out using your text editor and browser. You can save them as HTML files, place them into the HTML folder, and open them on your browser to see what those snippets of codes will do.

Your First HTML Page

Open your text editor and type the following in it:

Hello World!

After writing that line on your text editor, save it. On the save file dialog box, change the name of the file as firstexample.html. Do not forget the .html part. That part will serve as your file's file extension. It denotes that the file that you have saved is an HTML file and can be opened by the web browsers you have in your computer. Make sure that your program was able to save it as an .html file. Some text editor programs might still automatically add another file extension on your file name, so if that happens, you will not be open that file in your browser normally.

By the way, you do not need to upload your HTML file on a website or on the internet to view it. As long as your computer can access it, you can open it. And since your first HTML page will be in your computer, you can open it with your browser. After all, a web site can be viewed as a folder on the internet that contains HTML files that you can open.

When saving the file, make sure that it is being saved as plain text and not rich or formatted text. By default, programs such as Microsoft Word or WordPad save text files as formatted. If you saved the file as formatted, your browser might display the HTML code you have written incorrectly.

To open that file, you can try one of the three common ways. The first method is to double click or open the file normally. If you were able to save the file with the correct file extension, your computer will automatically open a browser to access the file.

The second method is to use the context menu (if you are using Windows). Right click on the file, and hover on the open with option. The menu will expand, and the list of programs that can open an HTML file will be displayed to you. Click on the browser that you want to use to open the file.

The third method is to open your browser. After that, type the local file address of your file. If you are using Windows 7 and you saved the file on the HTML folder in your desktop, then you can just type in C:\Users\User\Desktop\HTML\firstexample.html. The folder User may change depending on the account name you are using on your computer to login.

Once you have opened the file, it will show you the text you have written on it. Congratulations, you have already created a web page. You can just type paragraphs of text in the file, and it will be displayed by your browsers without problem. It is not the fanciest method, but it is the start of your journey to learn HTML.

You might be wondering, is it that easy? To be honest, yes. Were you expecting complex codes? Well, that will be tackled on the next chapter. And just to give you a heads up, it will not be complex.

This chapter has just given you an idea what is an HTML file and how you create, edit, and open one in your computer. The next chapter will discuss about tags, attributes, and elements.

Chapter 2: Elements, Properties, Tags, and Attributes

Of course, you might be already thinking: "Web pages do not contain text only, right?" Yes, you are right. In this part of the book, you will have a basic idea about how HTML code works, and how you can place some links on your page.

A web page is composed of elements. A picture on a website's gallery is an element. A paragraph on a website's article is also an element. A hyperlink that directs to another page is an element, too. But how can you do that with text alone? If you can create a web page by just using a text editor, how can you insert images on it?

Using Tags

Well, you can do that by using tags and attributes. By placing tags on the start and end of a text, you will be able to indicate what element it is. It might sound confusing, so below is an example for you to visualize and understand it better and faster:

<p>This is a paragraph that is enclosed on a paragraph tag. This is another sentence. And another sentence.</p>
In the example, the paragraph is enclosed with <p> and </p>. Those two are called HTML tags. If you enclose a block of text inside those two, the browser will understand that the block of text is a paragraph element.

Before you go in further about other HTML tags, take note that there is syntax to follow when enclosing text inside HTML tags. First, an HTML tag has two parts. The first part is the opening or starting tag. And the second part is the closing or ending tag.

The opening tag is enclosed on angled brackets or chevrons (the ones that you use to denote inequality – less and greater than signs). The closing tag, on the other hand, is also enclosed on angled brackets, but it includes a forward slash before the tag itself. The forward slash denotes that the tag is an ending tag.

Those two tags must come in pairs when you use them. However, there are HTML tags that do not require them. And they are called null or void tags. This will be discussed in another lesson. For now, stick on learning the usual HTML tags which require both opening and closing tags.

Attributes

When it comes to inserting images and links in your HTML file, you will need to use attributes. Elements have properties. The properties of each element may vary. For example, paragraph elements do not have the HREF property that anchor elements have (the HREF property and anchor element will be discussed shortly).

To change or edit those properties, you need to assign values using attributes tags. Remember, to indicate an element, use tags; to change values of the properties of elements, use attributes. However, the meanings and relations of those terms might change once you get past HTML and start learning doing CSS and JavaScript. Nevertheless, hold on to that basic idea first until you get further in web development.

Anyway, you will not actually use attributes, but you will need to indicate or assign values on them. Below is an example on how to insert a link on your web page that you will require you to assign a value on an attribute:

<a href="www.google.com" >Google</a>
If ever you copied that, pasted or written it on your HTML file, and open your file on a browser, you will see this:

Google

In the example above, the anchor or <a> HTML tag is used. Use the anchor tag when you want to embed a hyperlink or link in your page. Any text between the opening and closing tags of the anchor tag will become the text that will appear as the hyperlink. In the example, it is the word Google that is place between the tags and has appeared on the browser as the link.

You might have noticed the href="www.google.com" part. That part of the line determines on what page your link will direct to when you click it. That part is an example of attribute value assignment. HREF or hypertext reference is an attribute of the anchor tag.

By default, the anchor tag's value is "" or blank. In case that you do not assign any value to that attribute when you use the anchor tag, the anchor element will not become a hyperlink. Try copying and saving this line on your HTML file.

<a>Google</a>

When you open or refresh your HTML file, it will only show the word Google. It will not be underlined or will have a font color of blue. It will be just a regular text. If you hover on it, your mouse pointer will not change into the hand icon; if you click it, your browser will not do anything because the HREF value is blank.

By the way, when you assign a value on an element's or tag's attribute, you must follow proper syntax. The attribute value assignment must be inside the opening tag's chevrons and must be after the text inside the tag.

The attribute assignment must be separated from the tag with a space or spaces. The attribute's name must be type first. It must be followed by an equals sign. Then the value you want to assign to the attribute must follow the equals sign, and must be enclosed with double quotes or single quotes.

Take note, even if the number of spaces between the opening tag and the attribute assignment does not matter much, it is best that you only use one spaces for the sake of readability.

Also, you can place a space between the attribute name and the equals sign or a space between the equals sign and the value that you want to assign to the attribute. However, it is best to adhere to standard practice by not placing a space between them.

When it comes to the value that you want to assign, you can either enclosed them in double or single quotes, but you should never enclose them on a single quote and a double quote or vice versa. If you start with a single quote, end with a single quote, too. Using different quotes will bring problems to your code that will affect the way your browser will display your HTML file.

Nesting HTML Tags

What if you want to insert a link inside your paragraph? How can you do that? Well, in HTML, you can place or nest tags inside tags. Below is an example:

<p>This is a paragraph. If you want to go to Google, click this <a href="www.google.com" >link</a>.</p>

If you save that on your HTML file and open your file in your browser, it will appear like this:

This is a paragraph. If you want to go to Google, click this link.

When coding HTML, you will be nesting a lot of elements. Always remember that when nesting tags, never forget the location of the start and closing tags. Make sure that you always close the tags you insert inside a tag before closing the tag you are placing a tag inside on. If you get them mixed up, problems in your page's display will occur. Those tips might sound confusing, so below is an example of a mixed up tag:

<p>This is a paragraph. If you want to go to Google, click this <a href="www.google.com" >link</p>. And this is an example of tags getting mixed up and closed improperly.</a>

In the example, the closing tag for the paragraph tag came first before the closing tag of the anchor tag. If you copied, saved, and opened that, this is what you will get:

This is a paragraph. If you want to go to Google, click this link

. And this is an example of tag that was mixed up and closed improperly.

Since paragraphs are block elements (elements that will be always displayed on the next line and any element after them will be displayed on the next line), the last sentence was shifted to the next line. That is because the code has terminated the paragraph tag immediately.

Also, the anchor tag was closed on the end of the paragraph. Because of that, the word link up to the last word of the last sentence became a hyperlink. You should prevent that kind of mistakes, especially if you are going to code a huge HTML file and are using other complex tags that require a lot of nesting such as table tags. In addition, always be wary of the number of starting and ending tags you use. Missing tags or excess tags can also ruin your web page and fixing and looking for them is a pain.

This chapter has taught you the basic ideas about elements, properties, tags, and attributes. In coding HTML, you will be mostly fiddling around with them. In the next chapter, you will learn how to code a proper HTML document.

Chapter 3: The Standard Structure of HTML

As of now, all you can do are single lines on your HTML file. Though, you might have already tried making a page full of paragraphs and links – thanks to your new found knowledge about HTML tags and attributes. And you might be already hungry to learn more tags that you can use and attributes that you can assign values with.

However, before you tackle those tags and attributes, you should learn about the basic structure of an HTML document. The HTML file you have created is not following the standards of HTML. Even though it does work on your browser, it is not proper to just place random HTML tags on your web page on random places.

In this chapter, you will learn about the html, head, and body tags. And below is the standard structure of an HTML page where those three tags are used:

```
<!DOCTYPE html>
<html>
<head></head>
<body></body>
</html>
```

The Body and the Head

You can split an HTML document in two. The first part is composed of the things that the browser displays on your screen. And the second part is composed of the things that you will not see but is important to your document.

Call the first part as your HTML page's body. And call the second part as your HTML page's head. Every web page that you can see on the net are composed of these two parts. The tags that you have learned in the previous chapter are part of your HTML's body.

As you can see on the example, the head and body tag are nested inside the html tag. The head goes in first, while the body is the last one to appear. The order of the two is essential to your web page.

When coding in HTML, you should always place or nest all the tags or elements that your visitors will see on your HTML's body tag. On the other hand, any script or JavaScript code and styling line or CSS line that your visitors will not see must go into the head tag.

Scripts and styling lines must be read first by your browser. Even before the browser displays all the elements in your body tag, it must be already stylized and the scripts should be ready. And that is why the head tag goes first before the body.

If you place the styling lines on the end of the page, the browser may behave differently. For example, if the styling lines are placed at the end, the browser will display the elements on the screen first, and then once it reads the styling lines, the appearance of the page will change. On the other hand, if a button on your page gets clicked before the scripts for it was loaded because the scripts are placed on the end of the document, the browser will return an error.

Browsers and Checking the Source Code

Fortunately, if you forget to place the html, head, and body tags, modern browsers will automatically generate them for you. For example, try opening the HTML file that you created without the three tags with Google Chrome.

Once you open your file, press the F12 key to activate the developer console. As you can see, the html, head, and body tags were already generated for you in order to display your HTML file properly.

By the way, checking source codes is an important method that you should always use if you want to learn or imitate a website's HTML code. You can easily do it by using the developer console on Chrome or by using the context menu on other browsers and clicking on the View Page Source or View Source option.

Document Type Declaration

HTML has undergone multiple versions. As of now, the latest version is HTML5. With each version, some tags are introduced while some are deprecated. And some versions come with specifications that make them behave differently from each other. Because of that, HTML documents must include a document type declaration to make sure that your markup will be displayed just the way you wanted them to appear on your visitors' screens.

However, you do not need to worry about this a lot since it will certainly stick with HTML5, which will not be discussed in full in this book. In HTML5, document type declaration is useless, but is required. To satisfy this, all you need to do is place this on the beginning of your HTML files:

<!DOCTYPE html>

With all of those laid out, you can now create proper HTML documents. In the following chapters, the book will focus on providing you the tags that you will use the most while web developing.

Chapter 4: More HTML Tags

Now, it is time to make your HTML file to appear like a typical web page on the internet. And you can do that by learning the tags and attributes that are used in websites you stumble upon while you surf the web.

The Title Tag

First of all, you should give your web page a title. You can do that by using the <title> tag. The title of the page can be seen on the title bar and tab on your browser. If you bookmark your page, it will become the name of the bookmark. Also, it will appear on your taskbar if the page is active.

When using the title tag, place it inside the head tag. Below is an example:

```
<head>
        <title>This Is My New Web Page</title>
</head>
```

The Header Tags

If you want to organize the hierarchy of your titles and text on your web page's article, then you can take advantage of the header tags. If you place a line of text inside header tags, its formatting will change. Its font size will become bigger and its font weight (thickness) will become heavier. For example:

```
<h1> This Is the Title of This Article</h1>
<p>This is the introductory paragraph. This is another sentence. And this is the last sentence.</p>
```

If you try this example, this is what you will get:

This Is the Title of This Article

This is the introductory paragraph. This is another sentence. And this is the last sentence.

There are six levels of heading tags and they are: <h1>,<h2>,<h3>,<h4>,<h5>, and <h6>. Each level has different formatting. And as the level gets higher, the lesser formatting will be applied.

The Image Tag

First, start with pictures. You can insert pictures in your web page by using the <img> tag. By the way, the <img> tag is one of HTML tags that do not need closing tags, which are called null or empty tags. And for you to see how it works, check the example below:

<img
src="http://upload.wikimedia.org/wikipedia/commons/thumb/8/8o/Wikipedia
-logo-v2.svg/150px-Wikipedia-logo-v2.svg.png" >
If you try that code and opened your HTML file, the Wikipedia logo will appear. As you can see, the <img> tag did not need a closing tag to work. As long as you place a valid value on its src (source) attribute, then an image will appear on your page. In case an image file is not present on the URL you placed on the source attribute, then a broken image picture will appear instead.

Image Format Tips

By the way, the <img> tag can display pictures with the following file types: PNG, JPEG or JPG, and GIF. Each image type has characteristics that you can take advantage of. If you are going to post photographs, it is best to convert them to JPG file format. The JPG offers decent file compression that can reduce the size of your photographs without losing too much quality.

If you need lossless quality or if you want to display a photo or image as is, then you should use PNG. The biggest drawback on PNG is that old browsers cannot read PNG images. But that is almost a thing of a past since only handful people use old versions of browsers.

On the other hand, if you want animated images on your site, then use GIFs. However, take note that the quality of GIF is not that high. The number of colors it can display is few unlike PNG and JPG. But because of that, its size is comparatively smaller than the two formats, which is why some web developers convert their sites' logos as GIF to conserve space and reduce loading time.

The Ordered and Unordered List

Surely, you will place lists on your web pages sooner or later. In HTML, you can create two types of lists: ordered and unordered. Ordered lists generate alphanumeric characters to denote sequence on your list while unordered lists generate symbols that only change depending on the list level.

To create ordered lists, use the <ol> and <li> tag. The <ol> tag defines that the list will be an ordered one, and the <li> or list item tag defines that its content is considered a list item on the list. Below is an example:

<h1>Animals</h1>
<ol>
        <li>dog</li>
        <li>cat</li>
        <li>mouse</li>
</ol>
This will be the result of that example:

Animals

1. dog

2. cat

3. mouse

On the other hand, if you want an unordered list, you will need to use the <ul> tag. Like the <ol> tag, you will still need to use the <li> tag to denote the list items. Below is an example:

<h1>Verbs</h1>
<ul>
        <li>walk</li>
        <li>jog</li>
        <li>run</li>
</ul>
This will be the result of that example:

Verbs

• walk

• jog

- run

Instead of numbers, the list used bullets instead. If ever you use the <li> tag without <ol> or <ul>, browsers will usually create them as unordered lists.

Nesting Lists

You can nest lists in HTML to display child lists. If you do that, the browser will accommodate it and apply the necessary tabs for the child list items. If you nest unordered lists, the bullets will be changed to fit the child list items. Below is an example:

```
<h1>Daily Schedule</h1>
<ul>
        <li>Morning</li>

        <ul>
                <li>Jog</li>
                <li>Shower</li>
                <li>Breakfast</li>
        </ul>
        <li>Afternoon</li>
        <ul>
                <li>Lunch</li>
                <li>Watch TV</li>
        </ul>
        <li>Evening</li>
        <ul>
                <li>Dinner</li>
                <li>Sleep</li>
        </ul>
</ul>
```

This will be the result of that example:

Daily Schedule

- Morning

    o Jog

- Shower

- Breakfast

- Afternoon

  - Lunch

  - Watch TV

- Evening

  - Dinner

  - Sleep

And with that, you should be ready to create a decent website of your own. But for now, practice using those tags. And experiment with them.

Conclusion

Thank you again for purchasing this book!

I hope this book was able to help you to become knowledgeable when it comes to HTML development. With the fundamentals you have learned, you can easily explore the vast and enjoyable world of web development. And that is no exaggeration.

The next step is to learn more tags and check out websites' sources. Also, look for HTML development tips. Then learn more about HTML5 and schema markup. Those things will help you create richer web sites that are semantically optimized.

On the other hand, if you want to make your website to look cool, then you can jump straight to leaning CSS or Cascading Style Sheets. Cascading Style Sheets will allow you to define the appearance of all or each element in your web page. You can change font size, weight, color, and family of all the text on your page in a whim. You can even create simple animations that can make your website look modern and fancy.

If you want your website to be interactive, then you can start learning client side scripting with JavaScript or Jscript too. Scripts will provide your web pages with functions that can make it more alive. An example of a script function is when you press a button on your page, a small window will popup.

Once you master all of that, then it will be the best time for you to start learning server side scripting such as PHP or ASP. With server side scripting, you can almost perform everything on websites. You can take information from forms and save them to your database. Heck, you can even create dynamic web pages. Or even add chat functions on your website.

Finally, if you enjoyed this book, please take the time to share your thoughts and post a review on Amazon. We do our best to reach out to readers and provide the best value we can. Your positive review will help us achieve that. It'd be greatly appreciated!

Thank you and good luck!

Check Out My Other Books

Below you'll find some of my other popular books that are popular on Amazon and Kindle as well. Simply click on the links below to check them out. Alternatively, you can visit my author page on Amazon to see other work done by me.

C Programming Success in a Day

Android Programming in a Day

C Programming Professional Made Easy

C ++ Programming Success in a Day

Python Programming in a Day

PHP Programming Professional Made Easy

JavaScript Programming Made Easy

CSS Programming Professional Made Easy

Windows 8 Tips for Beginners

If the links do not work, for whatever reason, you can simply search for these titles on the Amazon website to find them.